ABBEYLEIX
THEN & NOW

ABBEYLEIX COMMUNITY GROUP

The
History
Press
Ireland

First published 2012

The History Press Ireland
50 City Quay
Dublin 2
Ireland
www.thehistorypress.ie

British Library Cataloguing in Publication Data.
A catalogue record for this book is available from the British Library.

ISBN 978 1 84588 751 3

Typesetting and origination by The History Press

CONTENTS

ACKNOWLEDGEMENTS

For contributions of photographs and information, our special thanks to Ruth Wallace, Brian Maher, Jim and Kathleen Fennelly, Nonie Duff, Philomena Flanagan, Tom Cox, Frankie Meehan, Paddy and Anne O'Hanlon, Miriam Wellwood and many other residents of Abbeyleix.

Abbeyleix Women's Development Group Ltd
Formed in 1999, Abbeyleix Women's Development Group Ltd is a socially inclusive group which encourages women to become active in their community. One of the group's aims is to encourage early school leavers to return to education and to provide affordable childcare. Under the drive and guidance of Mary White, the group published a book in 2008 entitled *Abbeyleix Our Town Our Lives* with reflections from various townspeople over the years.

James G. Carroll
A lifelong interest in photography and an immense pride in the history and development of Abbeyleix have led James Carroll to produce many stunning series of photographs of Abbeyleix and its surrounds over the years. His involvement in the production of this book has been immense, above and beyond the call of duty. At ceremonies and functions of every kind, James is present with his cameras to record the occasions, and so provides enduring memories for all concerned.

ABOUT THE AUTHOR

Kevin O'Brien comes from a family which has roots in Abbeyleix reaching back through at least four generations of O'Briens and Dooleys. He was born in 1937 near Windsor in Southern England. In 1946, his father brought his family back to Ireland to work on the de Vesci estate, where Kevin was brought up. He was educated by the Patrician Brothers and in 1958 graduated from University College Dublin with a Bachelor of Science degree. Kevin obtained a position as an electronic engineer with the Company of de Havilland Aircraft and worked on the guidance systems for rockets as part of the European Space Agency. On returning to Ireland in September 1961 to get married, he took up a post teaching science in Dundalk Grammar School and settled there with his wife Anne for the next twelve years.

Preferring to raise their family in a more rural setting, Anne and Kevin moved back to Abbeyleix in 1973 where Kevin continued to teach science in the nearby Salesian College at Heywood, Ballinakill, for the next twenty years until he retired on health grounds.

In the 1990s, Kevin O'Brien became a member of the Heritage Town local-history sub-committee. His interest in local history had been stimulated by the work of his late father, Pat O'Brien, who was an authority on local history. Kevin has written two books on local-history subjects. *Abbeyleix Golf Club, The First Hundred Years* was written on the occasion of the club's centenary in 1995. *Abbeyleix, Life, Lore and Legend* was published in 1998 and deals with the life and times of the town and surrounding area through the years.

In 2004, the O'More College of Design in Franklin, Tennessee, which has buildings known as Abbeyleix Mansions, established contact with Kevin to investigate the origin of the name. As this contact developed, the O'More College eventually incorporated a periodic Irish semester into their curriculum, where students and staff travel to Abbeyleix for courses involving tours around Ireland and lectures on Irish design, culture, and history. The County of Laois has been twinned with the County of Williamson, Tennessee in which O'More College is situated. For his work with this project, Kevin O'Brien has been made Professor of Irish History and Culture at O'More College, Franklin.

INTRODUCTION

In the second half of the twelfth century, the King of Leix was Conor O'More or Cochegerius O'More. In 1183, he was responsible for the foundation of a Cistercian abbey on the banks of the Nore. It became an institution of great standing which prospered for the next 400 years, so much so that for many centuries the land of Clonkeen at the south of the parish and the land around the abbey became known as Franamanagh, Land of the Monks.

Tradition in the area has maintained that the abbey was situated near, what is still known as, the Monks' Bridge across the Nore, and that the present-day Church of Ireland church on the local estate is built on the site of the Old Abbey church. As the years passed, the Cistercian monks began to employ farmers and labourers to assist them in their cultivation of the land and such like. These farmers and labourers brought their families and settled in houses and cabins near the abbey and on the abbey lands. They became tenants of the abbey and, in this way, the first village actually known as Abbeyleix developed close to the monastery.

For the next 400 years, the village of Abbeyleix developed beside the monastery with relatively little disturbance as the inhabitants were protected by the patronage of the abbey. Things changed, however, in 1542 when the abbey was suppressed and both the abbey and lands fell into the hands of the Ormond family of Kilkenny. In the years that followed, the village and surrounding lands changed hands many times as the O'Mores of Laois and the Ormonds and their allies fought for ownership of the area. Eventually, the lands and properties around Abbeyleix came into the hands of a speculator, Denny Muschamp, who, on the marriage of his daughter in 1699 to Sir Thomas Vesey, gave the couple the lands of Abbeyleix as a wedding present and thus started the development of the de Vesci Estate in Abbeyleix, making the de Vescis the landlords of the village.

Around the middle of the 1770s, the Viscount de Vesci of the time decided that the old village of Abbeyleix, which was situated on the marshy lands adjacent to the Nore, was too damp and unhealthy to be a place of habitation for his tenants. He started on the major project of moving an entire town and its inhabitants to a new site on higher ground, where the present-day town of Abbeyleix stands. This was the first example of the renovation of a town for the benefit of the tenants, and established Abbeyleix as a classical example of a planned estate town in Ireland. The old village was razed to the ground and very quickly the new town of Abbeyleix was established. It developed rapidly, to such an extent that the historian Sir Charles Coote describes the area in 1801 saying, 'Abbeyleix, lately established as a market town, a new and exceedingly neat village has arisen from its ruins [of the old village].' The core of the town was laid out more or less as it is today. The majority of the original houses were single-storey buildings, each with a thatched roof and a half-acre garden at the back. The lime trees planted down one side of the main street and the rippling stream flowing down the other side gave a uniquely serene atmosphere to the town from the beginning. Initially the town was known as New Rathmoyle, and then for a number of years as New Abbeyleix or simply New Town, before eventually becoming just Abbeyleix.

Along with the rest of the country, Abbeyleix suffered greatly during the time of the Famine and subsequent years. The building of the workhouse in the area of the modern district hospital relieved the situation somewhat, as did the benevolence of the de Vesci family who distributed flour and reduced rents during that time. However, hundreds died and many people were forced to emigrate.

In 1867, life in the town took a turn for the better with the coming of the railway. This linked the town to the major cities of the country and allowed the establishment of markets and fairs on a regular basis. This regular and speedy connection to the outside world had an enormous influence on the life of the town and its hinterland, and was of great commercial and economic benefit to the area. As a result, several projects developed in the town, such as a brewery, woollen mills, and Abbeyleix Lace and their produce was exported far and wide. The most notable industry was Abbeyleix Carpet Factory, which was set up in 1906 and became widely known for supplying carpets for the ill-fated sister ships, the *Brittanic*, the *Olympic*, and, most famous of all, the *Titanic*. Having been merged with Kildare Carpets in 1911, the Abbeyleix branch closed in 1912.

The first two decades of the twentieth century was a troublesome time for Abbeyleix. The First World War, the 1916 Rebellion, the War of Independence and the Civil War that followed all took their toll on the people of Abbeyleix and its surrounds. The 'flu epidemic of 1918 raged through the town and many townsfolk died during that year as a result.

Slowly the town began to recover and develop as shops and businesses appeared along Main Street. Various communal organisations, such as the ICA and Macra na Feirme were set up and flourished. Numbers attending the town's schools and churches grew, as, in spite of ongoing emigration, the population gradually increased. The 'Emergency' during the Second World War introduced rationing, and slowed growth for a period, but from then on the town grew in size as many new housing estates were built in the suburbs.

The 1990s saw the formation of the Heritage Company as the history and heritage of the town became appreciated to a greater degree. As a result, Abbeyleix acquired the national status of a Heritage Town with its long history displayed in the Heritage Centre for all to study.

THE OLD ESTATE CHURCH

THE OLD ESTATE Church of Ireland church which stands on the Abbeyleix Estate near the River Nore is believed to have been built on the site of the church of the old Cistercian abbey from which the town derives its name. The abbey flourished from its foundation in 1183 until its suppression in 1542 and was known as the Abbey of Leix. The nearby bridge over the Nore, known as the Monks' Bridge, is believed to have been built in the thirteenth century and was probably built by or under the direction of the Cistercian monks.

The Estate church served the community of the old village of Abbeyleix which had developed around the abbey. When, in the 1770s, the new town was developed on its present site, the Estate church was somewhat distant from the populace. As a result, in 1836, the present-day Church of Ireland church was built much closer to the town and the community. This new church was used for most ceremonies from 1840 onwards, although occasional services were held in the old church up until about 1950.

Emma, Viscountess de Vesci, wife of the third Viscount, was deeply involved in the development of the town of Abbeyleix during the nineteenth century, and was the driving force behind the building of schools and renovation of the churches in the town. The white marble tombstone in the old church is a fitting memorial to the Viscountess, who, being the daughter of the Earl of Pembroke, also gave the name to Pembroke Terrace. (*Images*: The Old Church, Abbeyleix Demense (left); The Church of Ireland church, 2011 (above).)

CHURCH OF ST MICHAEL AND ALL THE ANGELS

IT WAS VISCOUNTESS Emma de Vesci who organised a major renovation of the modern Church of Ireland church in the 1860s. This involved the dismantling of the older church except for the bell-tower and spire and the complete rebuilding of the structure under the direction of architect Mr Thomas Wyatt. The stained-glass windows in the new building, examples of the work of stained-glass artist Mr Henry Holiday, are particularly beautiful. The rector of Abbeyleix during many of these changes was Revd William Wingfield who, having been installed in 1836, served the parish with distinction for forty-four years, until his death in 1880.

At the end of the twentieth century, the church served the needs of both communities in Abbeyleix, when, on the occasion of the renovation of the Catholic church, the rector, Canon Patrick Harvey, and his community generously offered the use of the Church of Ireland church to

the Catholic community and for some eighteen months, the two communities shared the facilities there. (*Images*: Church of St Michael and All the Angels, *c.* 1950s (left); Church of St Michael and All the Angels, 2011 (above); Angel at the Birth of Christ (below left); The Archangel (below right).)

GLEN BAN SCHOOL

THE POWER OF education, a concept embraced in Abbeyleix from earliest times, may have been
a lingering influence from the days of the Cistercian monks. One of the most prominent of the
private schools in town was that of Miss Cora Mercier which eventually settled in Glen Ban. This
was a boarding school for young ladies. It catered for more than sixty boarders from all over
the province and also included a primary school for boys. The extensive grounds and gardens
ensured that the school was almost self sufficient. Pupils interested in riding were permitted
to bring their own ponies and stable them at the school during term time. The school uniform
was dark blue with gold trimmings and the school crocodile, two by two, wending its way down

to church or on a nature trail on the de Vesci estate, was a familiar sight in the town. At one stage, about 1935, it was planned to buy the mansion of Heywood House, near the town of Ballinakill, and transfer the school there, but these plans fell through. Eventually Glen Ban closed about 1940, shortly after the retirement of Miss Mercier. Thereafter Glen Ban house and lands moved into private hands and reverted to the world of farming and gardening. (*Images: Glen Ban School, 1910 (left); Glen Ban, 2011 (above).*)

BLUEGATE SCHOOLHOUSE

ABOUT A MILE south of the town of Abbeyleix stands Bluegate House, which started life as a gate lodge at an entry to the old de Vesci Estate. It was built about the middle of the nineteenth century, and stood beside, what was for many years, the main road from Dublin to Cork. Towards the end of that century, it was the home of a Miss Murphy who was a shining example of the enterprise and initiative typical of many Abbeyleix people during the first couple of decades of the last century. In many ways, Miss Murphy was almost 100 years ahead of her time, in that she operated what nowadays would be called a playschool or kindergarten for the very young children of the area. As soon as they could walk, the two and three year olds were taken to the schoolhouse, and were entertained and educated by Miss Murphy. Around 1920, as many as fifty toddlers attended Miss Murphy's playschool daily and were gently prepared for the life and times ahead of them.

A purpose-built extra room was added to the back of the house for the school. It had a large pot-bellied iron stove in the centre of the room with a metal chimney going almost to the ceiling and then across and out through the wall. The stove was completely surrounded with a rigid wire cage to protect the children and prevent accidents. All around the room ran a series of circular terraced benches and desks at which the youngsters were seated.

As well as the school, Miss Murphy was also involved in lace making and started the Abbeyleix Irish Knitting Industry and Abbeyleix Work School in Bluegate House and organised many of the local women as knitters in their own homes. In 1912, at the National Rural Industries Fair in Dublin, Stand 24 exhibited many beautiful embroidered frocks, which had been manufactured in the Work School in Bluegate House. Much of their produce was exported to England and America, and provided a very welcome additional income to many of the houses. It was unfortunate that when Miss Murphy retired in the middle 1920s, her school closed down and the knitting business faded away.

Bluegate House has been a private residence for many decades now. The schoolroom is still there, but the stove and the desks have long since gone. While the main entrance to the premises has been moved a short distance, the gate has been returned to its traditional blue from whence the immediate area acquired its name. (*Images:* Bluegate Schoolhouse, 1943 (above); Bluegate House, 2004 (left).)

15

METHODIST MANSE AND PRESBYTERIAN CHURCH

LOCAL TRADITION DESCRIBES how the Methodist Church came to the old village of Abbeyleix. Two gentlemen, Mr Leech and Mr White heard John Wesley preach in Mountrath and when Mr White came to live in the old village of Abbeyleix about 1753, he invited the Methodist preachers to conduct meetings in his house. A site for a chapel in the new town was leased by local members Joseph Dobbs, Thomas Kerr, Frederick Galbraith, and Jonathan Wilde amongst others. The chapel was built in 1826 and provided seats for 130 people. By 1850 a resident minister, Mr Thomas C. Laurance, was installed in the Manse which had been built on the adjoining plot of land. Over the door of the chapel was an unusual inscription: 'Can any good thing come out of Nazareth? Come and see.' At one of the services, local man Joseph Dobbs made a commitment to the church and, for more than fifty years, served with great faithfulness, developing the Methodist congregation

to such an extent that many quarterly meetings of the circuit were held in the town. The Methodist ministry went from strength to strength in the area and the Minister resident in Abbeyleix became responsible for Methodists in Durrow, Rathdowney and Donaghmore. The local Presbyterian community included the same regions, and established a church at Ballacolla.

In due course, the Manse and Epworth Hall were developed beside the main street. The hall derived its name from the village of Epworth in Lincolnshire, England where John Wesley, founder of Methodism, was born.

By the middle of the twentieth century, the once-thriving Methodist community had dwindled somewhat, and in 1948, the Abbeyleix Circuit was merged with the Carlow Circuit. Eventually in 1975, the community sold the Methodist Chapel to the Faith Mission who still make use of it to this day. During the war years, the shortage of petrol made it arduous for Presbyterians and their Minister to travel to their church in Ballacolla for services. Arrangements were made with the local Methodist community, and Presbyterian Services were held in the Methodist Epworth Hall, Abbeyleix, during those difficult times. Then as numbers dwindled, the Presbyterian church in Ballacolla was eventually demolished, and subsequently Presbyterian services were taken by Revd Fletcher in Mountmellick. (*Images:* Methodist Manse and Epworth Hall (left); Methodist Manse and Epworth Hall today (above).)

THE NORTH SCHOOL HERITAGE CENTRE

THE ORIGINAL SCHOOL building was constructed under the guidance of Lady Emma de Vesci and was completed in 1885. Its purpose was to provide primary education for the Catholic boys of the town and surrounds. It replaced a small overcrowded school at Stucker Hill on the main street. The new school was staffed by lay teachers and during the second and third decades of the twentieth century Mr Burchill and Mr Danny O'Sullivan ruled there with a firm hand. They were teachers in the old tradition and had served the town well for many years.

In 1934, however, after much debate, the Patrician Brothers were invited to take over the running of the North National School which they did for the next sixty years, and Mr Burchill and Danny O'Sullivan became part of the rich educational history of Abbeyleix. The stones from

the old Workhouse walls, which had been demolished in the early thirties, were used to build the extension to the North National School on the arrival of the Patrician Brothers.

The population of the town increased steadily over the years and plans for a new school eventually came to fruition with the completion of Scoil Mhuire on the Ballyroan Road in 1995. The old North National School was redundant, but survived to serve again in the future in a very different capacity. As the years rolled by, the richness of the town's history and heritage became recognised as a major asset. The Heritage Company succeeded in its purpose of having Abbeyleix designated as a Heritage Town, unique in being the first planned estate town in the country. and a Heritage Centre was opened in the old North National School, and is graced by a beautiful Cloidhna Cussen Sculpture near the entrance. In the centre it is possible to stroll through the ages, and to appreciate firsthand how history has moulded the town and its people. (*Images:* The North National School, *c.* 1910 (left); The Heritage Centre, 2011 (above).)

PRESTON HOUSE

TOWARDS THE END of the nineteenth century, the Preston House of today was known as the Assembly Rooms, provided by Viscount de Vesci as a place used for meetings, concerts and other public functions. In 1896, the endowed Preston School moved from Ballyroan into the Assembly Rooms. The Preston School was the subject of the longest litigation in British history, a dispute over finances lasting for over 100 years and the move to Abbeyleix was an indirect result of that law case. The building was extended to cater for the needs of the school and became known as Preston House. It operated as a non-denominational secondary school for many years.

In 1964, the new modern Vocational School along the Mountrath Road was completed and its first pupils were enrolled. The establishment of this school was the beginning of the end for the old Preston School, which had been declining in numbers for some years in spite of gallant efforts by Headmaster Mr Robert McShane. Sadly, the Preston School closed in 1966 after a long and troubled existence. Some students opted to attend boarding schools of their choice, particularly among the Church of Ireland community. Before long, the Salesian Fathers in Heywood opened their doors to local boys at second level with the Brigidine nuns catered for the girls of town.

The Preston went through a number of changes of purpose. For a while it became a series of flats or apartments, used mainly by young teachers or bank officials and the main hall was used as a meeting and concert hall. Eventually the main hall region was opened as a restaurant and remains so today. (*Images:* Preston School, *c.* 1955 (left); Preston House, 2011 (above).)

CHURCH OF
THE MOST HOLY ROSARY

IN 1893, THE old Catholic church on the hill was deemed inadequate for the numbers attending the ceremonies there and, with financial assistance from the de Vesci family and generous parishioner support, the present-day chapel was built under the guidance of the

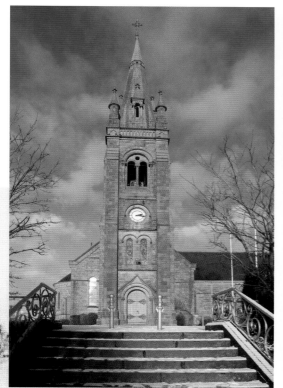

parish priest, the Revd James Lalor. The foundation stone was laid in 1893, and the main church of Irish-Romanesque design was completed by 1895. The bell tower and beautiful bell were added a year or two later. The architect was Mr Haigue, and the entire construction, including the magnificent internal decoration and beautiful stained-glass windows, was completed at a cost of £6,000. At the time of the centenary of the church, the parish priest, Revd Fr Patrick Kehoe, organised a major renovation of the interior of the building and of the church organ. During the time of renovation, the Church of Ireland Rector, Revd Patrick Harvey, and his community offered the use of their church to the Catholic congregation for the duration of the work. Their very generous offer was accepted with much gratitude, and for several months both communities prayed and worshipped in the beautiful Church of Ireland church, a very visible expression of the mutual respect and friendship of the people of Abbeyleix. (*Images:* Church of the Most Holy Rosary, *c.* 1895 without its spire (left); Church of the Most Holy Rosary, 2011 (above left); The Nativity Window (above right).)

SOUTH NATIONAL SCHOOL

LADY EMMA DE VESCI, wife of the third Viscount de Vesci, organised the building of the North and South National Schools during the second half of the nineteenth century. The South National School, originally built in 1843 and greatly extended in 1893, is one of the most elegant buildings in town. The style of building is very similar to that of many houses built by the de Vesci family over the years, particularly those built for many of the estate workers in various areas near town during the nineteenth century.

The similarity is very obvious in the original Killamuck cottages about two kilometres south of the town. These cottages exhibit the widespread use of cut limestone as the main building material of the cottages and the School, and the similar architectural overall design particularly the prominent ornamental timber facia boards. (*Images*: The South National School, *c.* 1910 (above); New School today (left).)

SOUTH NATIONAL SCHOOL

SITUATED AS IT is in a quiet and sylvan setting, this school building was at the centre of primary education for the Church of Ireland children for over 170 years. To the right of the school photograph are the classrooms and school facilities, while on the left is the school principal's living accommodation. The standard of education was excellent over the years and pupil numbers increased steadily necessitating many extensions, especially the major extension of 1893.

The new South Primary School is now in full use with all modern facilities. (*Images*: Pupils of South National School, 1913 (above); Pupils of Abbeyliex today (left).)

BRIGIDINE CONVENT

IN 1842, AT the request of the parish priest of the time, the Brigidine order of nuns came to Abbeyleix and founded the Brigidine Convent with the purpose of providing education for young girls from the surrounding area. The convent was built beside the old church. When the present church was built in 1893, the convent was linked to the new church by means of a convent chapel and the structure developed as can be seen in the photograph. The large white building contained the secondary school: classrooms, concert hall, etc., while the smaller building in front formed the primary school and school yard. The nuns catered for boarding pupils from all over the county and

beyond, and the building at the back on the left included dormitories, refectories and the like. The nuns' chapel can be seen towards the back, attached to the church. The schools flourished for over 100 years providing a tremendous service to the town and its hinterland.

Then, at the behest of the Department of Education, the primary school was amalgamated with the North School and the present-day Scoil Mhuire was founded. Next, the secondary school was merged with three other schools and moved to Heywood to form a Community School. Some of the nuns moved with the schools and continue to have an educational influence in both establishments. However, the buildings became redundant as the nuns moved to different accommodation, and in time both schools were demolished. The primary school area became a church car park and the secondary buildings were cleared and became a garden and social space for Dove House. The only remnant of what was once a great educational centre is the nuns' chapel which is still in regular use by the public to this day. (*Images*: Brigidine Convent, *c.* 1950 (left); Site of the convent, 2011 (above).)

THE HOSPITAL

THE ORIGINAL BUILDING on the site of the present district hospital was the Union Workhouse. The contract for building the Workhouse was signed in 1840, and it was designed to accommodate 500 'paupers'. The total cost was £6,900 and the work was finished early in 1844. With the onset of the Famine, it was soon full to capacity. In 1842, one wing of the Workhouse became a fever hospital to cope with the large number of illnesses brought on by malnutrition and poverty in the local population, especially in the Workhouse, during the Famine years and the years that followed.

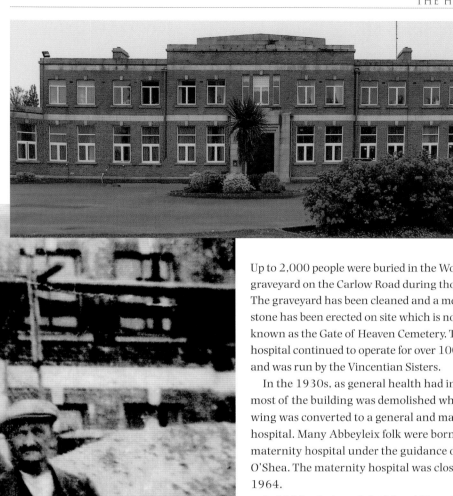

Up to 2,000 people were buried in the Workhouse graveyard on the Carlow Road during those years. The graveyard has been cleaned and a memorial stone has been erected on site which is now known as the Gate of Heaven Cemetery. The fever hospital continued to operate for over 100 years and was run by the Vincentian Sisters.

In the 1930s, as general health had improved, most of the building was demolished while one wing was converted to a general and maternity hospital. Many Abbeyleix folk were born in the maternity hospital under the guidance of Nurse O'Shea. The maternity hospital was closed in 1964.

In 1934, what was left of the old hospital and Workhouse were demolished and, on the arrival of the Patrician Brothers to the North School, the stones from the old Workhouse were used to build an extension to the existing school to provide the living quarters for the brothers.

The new district hospital was constructed in 1934. It caters for the old and infirm of the area who need more full-time nursing care than could otherwise be provided. Various other medical services are also available in the District Hospital such as physiotherapy and speech therapy. (*Images*: Men who worked on the building of Abbeyleix Hospital, 1934 (left); Abbeyleix District Hospital (above).)

KNOCKNAMOE HOUSE

KNOCKNAMOE HOUSE WAS built in 1841 by the second Viscount de Vesci, as part of a twenty-five-house complex, known as Temperance Street, for rental to elderly people and widows at a minimum rent. It was used for this purpose throughout the years until 1968, when it was handed over to the care of the County Council. A shortage in County Council finances meant that over the years many of the houses fell into disrepair, Knocknamoe House being one of them. As the town progressed to its status as a heritage town, the decision was made to renovate the house and, in due course, the house was restored to its present condition.
(*Images*: Knocknamoe House in disrepair, 1980 (left); Knocknamoe House, 2011 (above).)

DOVE
HOUSE
GARDENS

PART OF THE old grounds of the
convent was developed during the
1990s under the auspices of the
Horizon Employment Initiative of
the European Union. The Sisters of
Charity of Jesus and Mary had started
Dove House, their day programme
and the sheltered unit for the care
and education of those of intellectual
disability in the old Vocational School
building on the Mountrath Road.

In 1995, they moved to the new
purpose-built centre in the old convent

garden with access provided from Upper Main Street. Associated with the centre is the Abbey Sensory Garden, elegantly designed for sensory stimulation and interest, and providing an oasis of peace and tranquillity for one and all. The garden was officially opened in 1997 by President Mary Robinson.

Apart from being a quiet and convenient haven for a moment's reflection for any passer-by, the garden is a beautiful open-air classroom for the staff and students of Dove House. Appreciation of nature and general maintenance of gardens are among the many subjects explored and enjoyed by all.

A visit to Dove House and its gardens can be a most gratifying and inspirational experience at any time of year, but especially so during spring and summer when nature can be seen in all it glory. (*Images*: Convent Gardens (above); Dove House Gardens today (left).)

LABURNUM LODGE

LABURNUM LODGE IS a stately two-storey house built beside the Ballyroan Road on the northern side of town. During the third decade of the twentieth century, it was the property of the Finnegan family, and because of its situation it became a very strategic position during the Civil War in Abbeyleix. It was commandeered by the Free State soldiers during the battle for control of the town, as from the upper bedroom windows they had an uninterrupted view in those days, of the Courthouse and the main street. In the interest of their safety, the Finnegan family moved up to Rathmoyle House on the invitation of the Wilde family, and they joined many

of the Rathmoyle residents who had gathered in and around Rathmoyle House for their own protection. The house was set well back from the road, and was therefore out of harm's way to some extent. The Free State soldiers stationed in Laburnum Lodge exchanged sporadic rifle fire with the Republicans who were based in the Courthouse. In the process, much damage was done both inside and outside the lodge. One young soldier named Glynn was shot at the gate of the lodge and later died of his injuries.

After the Civil War, the lodge was acquired by the Brigidine nuns, and was used as a school for a number of years, after which Laburnum Lodge passed into private hands. (*Images*: Laburnum Lodge, *c.* 1920 (left); Laburnum Lodge, 2011 (above).)

THE MARKET HOUSE

THE MARKET HOUSE was built in 1836 by the second Viscount de Vesci. It is just off the main street of the town and surrounded behind by a semi-circle of shops and houses. The original building, used mainly for marketing purposes particularly on market and fair days, had five bay openings on the main road side. In addition, there were two projecting single-storey structures which were used mainly as butcher stalls.

In 1906, the building was renovated and enlarged as a memorial to the fourth Viscount de Vesci. In essence a second storey was added which was used as a meeting place and a dance and concert hall. On occasion during the 1920s and '30s, it was used as a cinema whenever films became available. Around 1950, the building became the property of Laois County Council, who in time converted the ground floor into the town's fire station and the upper floor into a library.

Then, in 2006, when a new purpose-built fire station was constructed on the Portlaoise Road, the entire building was renovated again and became a very modern computerised public library, which provides a wide range of amenities and functions for the public of Abbeyleix. (*Images*: Town Hall and Market House on Fair Day *c.* 1900 (left), The Market House as a library, 2011 (below).)

SEXTON'S HOUSE

ONE OF THE excellent projects undertaken by the Heritage
Company has been the renovation of the Sexton's House. For
a number of generations, the office of Sexton to the Church of
Ireland church was held by members of the Galbraith family
who served the church and its congregation admirably over

the years. Among the many duties to be performed was one which all of the residents of Abbeyleix appreciated was the ringing of the church bell to welcome in the New Year at midnight. Many an emigrant, on hearing a church bell, wherever they might be, would be swept back home on a wave of nostalgic feeling.

On the retirement of the last sexton the house became somewhat derelict and, as it forms a significant part of the town's heritage, its restoration was widely welcomed. It is now a notable stop on the heritage trails around the town (*Images*: The Sexton's House before renovation (above); The Galbraith Family *c.* 1939 (above left); The Restored Sexton's House (below left).)

THORNBERRY HOUSE

THORNBERRY (ALSO KNOWN as Thornbury and Thornbay) House was built early in the nineteenth century and was owned by Richard Crocker who was a captain in the British Navy and one of the gentry of the time. Richard Crocker was married to Catherine Jane Bland QC and, when he died in 1836, the property passed into the hands of the Bailey family. In 1846, Wellesley C. Bailey was born in Thornberry House and after a number of adventures he happened to visit a leper mission in India, and was so deeply affected by their plight that he dedicated the rest

of his life to helping them, eventually founding the society Missions to Lepers in India. He worked tirelessly with this society until his death in 1937 at the age of ninety-one.

In the early years of the twentieth century, Thornberry House stood beside what is now a housing estate of the same name. It was a fine house which became the home of a wealthy family, the Waldrons. By all accounts, it was a prosperous household which provided employment for a large number of housemaids, cooks and so on. The Waldrons were very much of the gentry class and socialised with the de Vesci family and similar families.

When Mr Waldron died, his wife and family moved to England and Thornberry House was sold to Fintan Phelan, a local man who had a thriving business in town: a public house and grocery store at the Corner House in the centre of town.

Sadly, during the second part of the twentieth century, Thornberry House became vacant and fell into disrepair and the remaining structure was demolished in the interests of safety. (*Images*: Thornberry House, c. 1910 (below); Mr John Waldron of Thornberry House (below left); Site of Thornberry House, 2011 (above left).)

DE VESCI ARMS HOTEL

IN ITS EARLIEST days, the de Vesci Arms Hotel was a coach office and staging post for the famous Bianconi stage coaches of the eighteenth and nineteenth centuries. Stage coaches from Dublin travelling towards the towns and cities in the south of the country used the hotel as a stop for a change of horses or for an overnight stay on longer journeys. During its long history, the hotel had been the main place of rest in town for weary travellers. Both Daniel O'Connell and British Prime Minister Gladstone stayed there on occasion, according to legend.

The location of the hotel, being in the very centre of town, was of great value to the shops and business premises in the town and a source of employment for blacksmiths, stable lads, and such like, along with the many who worked and served in the hotel itself.

While the coming of the railway in 1866 was of enormous benefit to the town in general, it seriously impacted on the economics of the hotel. Gradually the Bianconi coaches disappeared from the scene, now that a trip by coach, which might have taken a couple of days, could be completed in hours by train. With the loss of the coach trade, business and employment at the hotel was diminished. The premises was purchased by the Morrissey family of Abbeyleix around the turn of the century and continued to operate as a hotel for many years. Morrisseys converted part of the hotel to a drapery store for a while with considerable success as can be seen in the 1910 photo.

During the twentieth century, the drapery shop closed and the premises continued as a hotel for many years under changing management. The emphasis of business altered as the years past. The building became a Folkhouse and a concert centre, among other things, eventually becoming The Abbeygate as it is today. (*Images*: The de Vesci Arms Hotel *c.* 1910 (below); The Abbeygate, 2011 (left).)

FIRE BRIGADE

JUST AFTER THE Second World War, the town acquired its own branch of the Fire Brigade which has served the community so well over the years. One of its first major challenges came in January 1950, when Heywood House near Ballinakill was destroyed by fire. At that time the house was the novitiate for the Irish province of the Salesian Fathers and many from Abbeyleix provided help and accommodation to the priests and their pupils during the following years as the Salesians slowly recovered from their loss. Since those early years, the local brigade has availed of every opportunity to improve its fire-fighting ability both in terms of equipment and manpower, and today, thanks to the drive and determination of those like the late Christy Phelan, the town has a fire brigade of which it can be proud and in which it has great confidence. (*Images:* Fire Brigade (above); Modern Fire Brigade (below left); Fire Officer Tim Bonham introduces the fourth successive Bonham generation to the fire service (above left).)

THE FIRE STATION

THE ORIGINAL FIRE Brigade Station was situated on the Mountrath Road. The building was small and unimpressive but catered for the limited equipment available at the time for this very essential service. As the service developed, the premises were improved to match. Space remained very limited however. When larger machines and equipment were acquired, a move became necessary and the lower storey of the Town Hall of the time was acquired. The premises was equipped with the very latest of technology and served the brigade and the townsfolk with distinction for many years.

Finally, it was felt that the brigade needed purpose-built premises and the modern-day Fire Station was built on the Portlaoise Road, just outside town. (*Images*: The Old Fire Station (above); The Old Station Restored (left).)

LOWER MAIN STREET

LOWER MAIN STREET in 1906. The photo shows many points of interest. There is the town stream which flowed gently through the town and was crossed by a number of small bridges which allowed access to the path and the shops. The stream was a source of fun for young folk coming home from school who floated their paper boats in a race to see whose would go faster. In the 1960s, the stream was piped and covered on safety grounds, a cause of great sadness on the part of many Abbeyleix people who felt the town lost part of its unique character. Also visible in the 1906 picture are two of the telephone poles to which the wires for the new telephone service would be attached in due course. The town's famous lime trees line the street along the left. One of the paraffin street lamps can be seen

standing beside the stream towards the right. These lamps were lit by hand at dusk each evening. The copper dome of the Bank of Ireland can be seen just right of centre. A busy day in town and only one car in sight partially hidden by the horse and cart in foreground.

A cloudy day in Abbeyleix 2011. The stream is long underground, the large lime trees were removed during the late nineties as they had become very old and somewhat dangerous. They have been replaced this time on both sides of the road by young limes which, with a bit of luck, will last over 100 years as their predecessors did. The Main Street was completely modernised in 1999 as befits a heritage town. All the wires, telephone and electricity etc., have disappeared underground and the broad wide street has been narrowed to make way for parking along the street on each side. The new street lamps too are of heritage design and frame the street beautifully. Since the motorway from Dublin to Cork opened a few years ago, traffic is considerably reduced, leaving a quiet elegant heritage town. The photo shows a typical weekday morning view of the street and not a pony in sight. (Lower Main Street, Abbeyleix, 1906 (left); Lower Main Street, Abbeyleix, 2011 (above).)

MEEHAN'S AND ALLIED IRISH BANKS

MEEHAN'S DRAPERY STORE was in its time a very impressive building at the bottom of the Chapel Avenue. As an elegant drapery store, it carried an enormous range of goods to suit every taste and fashion. During the early years of the twentieth century, it was a major focal point for shoppers in Abbeyleix and the surrounding regions. Being across the street from the de Vesci Arms Hotel, a Bianconi coach stop, it was in a prime position to be of service to the travelling public who frequented the hotel, in the days when most road traffic was horse-drawn and longer journeys required a number of hotel stops along the way.

As time went by, the train became the more common form of travel and other more modern shops in the town began to develop. As a result, the old-fashioned drapery store became less popular and business began to fade.

Eventually the store closed and the premises became the Munster and Leinster Bank, one of the new banks which developed rapidly in the newly independent state. This bank thrived for many years until a merger with other banks lead to the formation of the Allied Irish Banks, in the middle of the century. The old paraffin lamp outside the building has been replaced by the new heritage lighting system, and the old-style postbox has also disappeared, being replaced with the postbox in the wall of the post office. The imposing shop front has been changed and been replaced, for security purposes, by a very solid wall.

To this day, the Allied Irish Banks serves the populace of the town and surrounding hinterland in an imposing and elegant edifice. (*Images*: Meehan's Drapery Store, *c*. 1900 (left); Allied Irish Banks, Abbeyleix 2011 (above).)

BROPHYS'

UNTIL 1910, AN old Abbeyleix family, the Brophys, lived in what is now the town's post office. The post office moved from Pembroke Terrace into its present location about 1910, and the Brophy family, who had been running a public house there, moved to the corner shop at the bottom of the chapel avenue. Three of the Brophy sisters, Josie, Bessie, and Rita, established a newsagent's and sweet shop there, which for the next seventy-odd years was an institution in the town, a centre of activity and information. The shop was a magnet for every schoolchild of those generations, providing everything needed for school life: copies, pens, rulers, and a choice of so many sweet delights from penny gobstoppers to an assortment of ice cream.

The daily national and local papers were sold there, and the headlines of the day were the topic of conversation among the many customers both within the shop and on pavements outside. So many of the country's problems were solved over and over again in and around Brophys' shop, the problem was that those governing the country were not there to listen and learn. The shop's situation was ideal in that it was close to the convent schools and on the way to the North National School, and a large part of the trade depended on the passing schoolchildren. When the convent schools closed and the new school Scoil Mhuire opened, the majority of pupils were taken by car to the new school meaning the trade of the shop suffered.

As the Brophy sisters retired, the shop was taken over by various people and continued as a newsagent until the end of the twentieth century when it was bought out and converted into a café, first as the Café Odhran, and now as Savour. It is still great spot for refreshment and a quiet chat for townsfolk and traveller alike, and while the hum of activity of myriads of schoolchildren at school time is now just a memory, the café has embarked on the business of creating its own rich memories for future generations. (*Images*: Brophys' Newsagent, *c*. 1965 (left); Savour Café today (above).)

FYFFE'S

ON THE WESTERN side of The Square, Fyffe's Drapery has become an institution in Abbeyleix and has been for over a century. Several generations of the family have served the people of the town with distinction. Some aspects of shop life have changed, as can be seen in the photographs. Methods of displaying wares, for example, have changed radically. One hundred years ago, items were laid out on pathways and hung from shop fronts, provided the weather allowed, whereas these days much of the advertising is done through papers, newsletters and especially on the internet.

Fyffe's can only benefit also from the development of the ultra-modern library virtually on their doorstep, and from the weekly Farmers' Market held on Saturdays, both of which draw prospective customers to that side of the Market square. The provision of car parking spaces in the vicinity of the shop is also of value. (*Images*: Fyffe's, *c.* 1900 (left); Fyffe's 2011 (above).)

MORRISSEY'S

WHEN THE NEW town of Abbeyleix was built in the late 1770s, one of the first families to move into a building in town was the Morrissey family, who opened a combined grocery shop and public house. Over the years, the business flourished and expanded into the fields of travel agency, auctioneering, and funeral directors. The policy of the proprietors, such as the late Paddy Mulhall, was to maintain the traditional atmosphere of the place as far as possible, and by doing so Morrisseys gained worldwide fame as a tourist attraction, and was recognised in the top-ten international public houses for several years. Among the many policies that merited praise was the policy of assisting emigrants, particularly those going to America, by giving them £5 from Viscount de Vesci and a stamped addressed postcard to be posted by them when they arrived in New York. In this way, those at home knew they had arrived safely. Another practice for the benefit of

locals involved leaving one timber shutter in place on each window during the day whenever a death had occurred in the locality and enquiries inside would determine who had passed on. The business remained in the Morrissey family until the end of the twentieth century. (*Images*: Morrissey's in the 1960s (left); Morrissey's stalwarts Eleanor Thornton and Paddy Mulhall (below); Morrissey's, 2011 (above).)

PEMBROKE TERRACE

FROM AN ARCHAEOLOGICAL perspective, Pembroke Terrace, which is situated near the southern end of the town, is one of the most significant buildings in the town. It was built in the 1830s as part of the dowry of Emma, daughter of Lord Pembroke, who had married Thomas Vesey, the third Viscount de Vesci during the first half of the 1830s. Emma was the granddaughter of Count Worenzov, and she modelled much of the terraced gardens at Abbeyleix House on those of her grandfather at Alupca near Yalta in the Crimea. It was Emma, along with her husband, Lord Thomas de Vesci, who financed and organised the installation of piped water in the Workhouse in 1874 and later extended the scheme to cover most of the town, including Pembroke Terrace, making it one of the first towns in the country to have water on tap.

During the second half of the nineteenth century, the four houses of the terrace were occupied by the post office, the police station, the police sergeant's house and a bank, later known as the Hibernian Bank. During the early years of the twentieth century the occupancy changed. In 1906, the Hibernian Bank moved to new premises, the site of the present-day Bank of Ireland. The post office moved in 1910 to its present position in the square, and by the middle of the century the police, which by now had become the Gardaí, moved to a new purpose-built building on the Ballinakill Road. The Hibernian Bank's old property was developed as a hotel, and not surprisingly was named the Hibernian Hotel. The other three buildings passed into private hands as they remain today. In recent years, the hotel closed and is being used currently to house immigrant families while their applications for residency are being processed. (*Images*: Pembroke Terrace, *c.* 1906 (left); Pembroke Terrace today (below).)

THE TOWN PARK

IN THE EARLY part of the twentieth century, the need for a park in Abbeyleix was recognised by Revd Fr Breen, the parish priest of the time. Behind the shops and houses of Main Street and to the west of town, was a large gravel pit known as Jelly's Pit. Fr Breen decided that the pit could be transformed into a town park and set about organising the transformation. A large number of volunteer workers were persuaded to take part in what is known as 'The Big Push'. Using picks, spades and shovels, the townsfolk swept into the pit, and in a very short period of time, it was transformed into a large area of grass surrounded by a grassy bank. In a gesture of honour and appreciation, the park was named the Fr Breen Park.

The tennis club was already in residence in one corner and the local GAA teams began to play their matches regularly in the park. Slowly, over the years, other sports began to make use of the pitch. Marquees were erected on special occasions and carnivals and dances organised. Many a romance started in and around such marquees, even if a somewhat overbearing supervision was compulsory in the early days.

In time, a fine hall was built known today as the CYMS Hall and was available for a great variety of functions, and with the provision of changing rooms and so on, the park developed into the wonderful facility it is today. (*Images:* The Big Push, *c.* 1930 (left); Revd Fr Breen Park today (above).)

THORNTON'S BAKERY

AT VARIOUS TIMES during the first half of the twentieth century, up to seven bakeries flourished in Abbeyleix. One of the more enduring was Thornton's Bakery on the Ballinakill Road, which, as can be seen in the photograph, possessed one of the very first delivery vans in town. It was a great

adventure in those early days for any youngster in town to get even a short trip in the van. As the years passed, the standard of van improved, whereas the standard of product was always excellent with a reputation second to none in the area. For the people of Abbeyleix and its surrounds, Thornton's crisp crusty pan loaves were a joy to behold and to savour. In passing Thornton's bread van making deliveries on the early morning Main Street, the mouth-watering aroma of warm fresh bread would engulf the passer-by. Some were known on occasion, to walk up and down past the van just to prolong the delicious experience. With the advent of the national bakeries and the better transport for delivery to supermarkets etc. Thornton's, like many other local businesses, closed down and the premises has become a private home. (*Images*: Thornton's Bakery (left); Thornton's Bakery today (above).)

UPPER MAIN STREET

ON THE NORTHERN side of the town, Upper Main Street has always tended to be of a more residential character than the lower part of the street. The old North School can be seen at the top of the town and the gentle rise in the road leading up to it has always been known as Stucker Hill. Before the North School was built in 1885, a small primary school for boys existed on the left-hand side of Stucker Hill, while on the opposite side, was the coach building firm of Crennans'. This family concern was started in 1845 by Michael Crennan. At times it employed over thirty people including carpenters, blacksmiths and painters, and they built a superb reputation in the craft of coach building. This side of the business was to continue successfully until the advent of the motor car in the late 1920s. Shortly after it closed, a terrace of houses was built which was known as the New Terrace.

Coming down the hill towards the square, on the left side, were mainly dwelling houses, although a number of small family businesses were carried on by the occupants, tailoring, dressmaking, a saddlery, and later petrol pumps. On the right side, below the new terrace, some shops and a motor garage developed, ending with Brophys' Newsagents at the corner of the Chapel Avenue.

In modern times, on this side of the street, the greatest change was the establishment of Dove House with the Sensory Gardens. The introduction of the heritage street lighting in 2000, and the removal of overhead wiring along with the reduction of through traffic, has restored the street to its peaceful elegance of bygone days. (*Images*: Upper Main Street, *c*. 1910 (below); Upper Main Street, 2011 (left).)

KNOCKNAMOE PARK

FOR A NUMBER of years, the small area of land beside
Knocknamoe House on the Ballinakill Road, looked
like a forlorn forgotten field. As time passed, the field
became an eyesore and seemed to collect more rubbish,

in spite of efforts to tidy the region from time to time. Then, with the Tidy Towns Competition generating more and more interest in the town, it was decided to do something positive with the area. It was developed into a small park with the necessary amenities to provide a scenic and relatively peaceful facility, where the passer-by could relax, rest and unwind for a few minutes.

The result is a delight to behold, graced as it is with a Cliodna Cussen Sculpture, forming the entry style beside the footpath. (*Images*: Knocknamoe Park (above); Knocknamoe Park today (below left); Cliodhna Cussen Sculpture (above left).)

69

ABBEYLEIX CARPET FACTORY

THE ABBEYLEIX CARPET FACTORY was set up by Lord de Vesci in 1904 to improve the employment situation and to reduce the number of people who were being forced to emigrate. Up to forty women and girls were employed in the Carpet Factory, which had been built in the centre of town, behind what became Bramley's Motor Works and is now Weaver Court. The name of Abbeyleix Carpets became known worldwide. Up until 1912, many magnificent carpets were manufactured and distributed to all parts of the world, the most famous being the carpets for the tragic *Titanic* and her sister ships the *Olympic* and *Britannic*, all three of which had been fitted with Abbeyleix carpets before their maiden voyages. Sadly, having amalgamated with the Kildare Carpet Company, the Abbeyleix branch was closed in late 1912.

The carpet factory stood some way back from the Main Street of the town and not long after its closure, the Bramley family built the Abbeyleix Motor Works on the site. The garage and petrol pump facility operated successfully and served local and passing trade for many years before closing down at the end of the century.

In place of the motor works, a block of apartments have been built, known appropriately as Weaver Court, providing homes for many in the centre of town. A Heritage Company information sign over the entrance to Weaver Court marks the site of the old carpet factory. (*Images*: Carpet Factory under construction, *c.* 1905 (above); Weaver Court 2011 (left).)

SCHOOL OF DANCING

DURING THE 1950s, a highly talented young Abbeyleix girl embarked on a career which was to earn her and her hometown worldwide recognition. Maura Bonham, later to become Mrs Shanahan, decided to share her wonderful talent for music and dance with the young people of the town and surrounding districts and started her Irish Dancing School, Scoil Rince Bonnean. Almost immediately, Maura and her pupils made a profound impression on the world of Irish music and dance and, together with one of her gifted music pupils, Jimmy Hartford, she set the exceptionally high standards to which others would aspire. In the early years, everything was on a small scale. The costumes were simple yet elegant, the style of dancing was very traditional, and the button accordion of maestro Jimmy Hartford was the

only source of music. However, from such small beginnings Maura Shanahan's School of Music and Dance would develop and grow to virtually encompass the world.

In fact, by the turn of the century, Maura Shanahan was putting the name of Abbeyleix on the worldwide folk music and dance map, as her Scoil Rince of the 1950s had blossomed into the School of Music Song Folklore and Folkdance. For more than forty-five years, Maura has diligently served the community in the field of music and dance, and has taken many of her pupils, who now come from all over Laois and Offaly, to folk festivals in every corner of the world with great success. Her great knowledge and enthusiasm for every aspect of Irish folk culture, earned her numerous initiative and cultural awards from all over the globe. Having taught Irish dancing and music in places as far apart as Russia and Slovakia, Maura became the National Chairperson of the Council of International Folklore Festivals and has been an Irish delegate to the General World Assembly of CIOFF for many years. From the design of the beautiful costumes to the exhilaration of the dance, the late Maura Shanahan's hand guided her musicians and dancers to the pinnacle of success. (*Images*: The Bonham School of Dance, 1970s (left); The Shanahan School of Folklore and Folkdance, 1995 (above).)

HIGH NELLIE CLUB

THE BICYCLE WAS a very common form of transport during the middle years of the last century, but as motor transport became cheaper and more widespread, the use of bikes faded in popularity. The protection from the weather when in a car was a great advance, allowing more comfort and creating the possibility of a much wider range of travel.

On occasion, back in the 1940s and '50s, the bicycle was used for more than the mundane trip into town for shopping. The archive image, taken about the late 1960s, shows a charity marathon ride by the ladies of the Abbeyleix Irish Countrywomen' sAssociation (ICA). Apparently, they undertook to ride from Abbeyleix to Durrow, then on to Ballacolla and eventually back to Abbeyleix, with stops for refreshments in both towns. When the road-surface condition of the time is taken into consideration, the journey truly was a marathon.

In modern times, with the success of vintage car groups and veteran tractor associations, the old-style bike is coming to the fore again. Christened the High Nelly, the old-style bike is reasserting itself. This time both men and women are indulging in bouts of nostalgia, again in charitable causes, and are taking to the roads, and benefiting from the exercise as well as helping the needy. (*Images*: Abbeyleix ICA, *c.* late 1960s (above); High Nelly Club, 2011 (left).)

MACRA NA FEIRME

ON 16 APRIL 1948, at a meeting of young farmers of the area, the Abbeyleix branch of Macra na Feirme came into being on a proposal of Sean Reilly. Mr Tom Casey became the first president of the branch.

Sean Reilly was secretary for eighteen years, before becoming president of the branch. The principal purpose of Macra na Feirme was educational and to make available to all, the latest advances in every aspect of agricultural life. The local group, driven by the enthusiasm of its founder members, blossomed into a forceful and ambitious branch, reaching a membership of over 100 during

the 1950s, and widening the scope of its interests into the fields of public speaking, drama and debate, with great success. Meetings were held every fortnight, and the forest of bicycles outside the meeting house was a sight to behold. There was one car, that of Dick Palmer, who was treasurer of the branch for many years.

Before long, the members realised that they needed a home of their own, and such was their drive and ambition that in a short period of time they had raised the sum of £5,000 and had built the impressive Macra Hall just off the Mountrath Road, which was to serve their needs and provide a marvellous facility for the town for the next forty years or so.

The first sod on the site was cut by Bride Reilly and George Galbraith in 1958.

Towards the end of the last century, use of the Macra Hall declined to such an extent that it closed as a community hall and became a base for a grass-cutting industry, and storage for machinery. In later years, the hall was demolished and developed as a housing estate.
(*Images*: The Macra Hall, *c*. 1990 (above); Macra Na Feirme, 1953 (above left); Site of Macra Hall today (below left).)

ABBEYLEIX GOLF CLUB

SINCE ITS FOUNDATION in 1895, Abbeyleix Golf Club has played an ever-increasing role in the social life of the community of the town and its surrounds. The club has the distinction of being one of the oldest clubs in Ireland. Its membership around the beginning of the twentieth century was small and tended to come from the more affluent members of the town. Little is known of the officers of the early years of the club, as many of the committee books of the era have been mislaid. Throughout the early years, the club president and patron was Viscount de Vesci. The first record of a captain is in 1905 when a Mr R. Hampton held the office. It was in 1905 that the club became affiliated with the Golfing Union

of Ireland. Mrs J. Cunningham, the first lady captain, appears in 1949. For the first fifty years of its existence, two general impressions of the membership can be gleaned from newspaper reports and surviving minute books. The first is that the early members of the club were nothing if not persistent and determined survivors. The second impression is that the name 'Wanderers' in their title might have been appropriate as, in their determination to survive, the members used a variety of courses in the surrounds of Abbeyleix and just beyond. The first photo shows the members on Captain's Day 1932 with captain, Mr R. Fyffe front centre, when the course was situated in Ballymullen to the south of the town. With the onset of the Second World War, the club became dormant, until, in the late 1940s, some of the members renewed their golfing activities on a nine-hole course in Rathmoyle and from then on the membership has continued to grow and the club has thrived.

In 1995, the club enjoyed its centenary with a year filled with celebratory activities of many descriptions, beginning with the drive-in in appropriate historical dress. Membership increased dramatically and people drawn from all walks of life joined the club during the end of the century, and, as the new millennium dawned, the club extended the course to eighteen holes to accommodate the larger membership. The nature of the club has changed over the years as circumstances have changed. The screening of golf on the television and the success of Irish professional golfers internationally has created a keen interest in the game, particularly among the youth of the town and augers well for the future of Abbeyleix Golf Club. (*Images*: Golf members, 1932 (below); Golf members, 1995 centenary (left).)

THE ICA

IN 1914, A branch of the Irish Countrywomen's Association (ICA) was started in Abbeyleix for the first time, and from small beginnings developed into one of the most influential groups in town. Canon Neville's wife Rosetta, who died in 1963, had been a driving force in the ranks of the ICA for many years and had helped to develop that organisation into a wonderful amenity for the ladies with great influence on town and country life in the region. There is no doubt that Rosetta would have revelled in the celebrations in 1964 when the local branch of the ICA marked the fiftieth anniversary of its foundation in fine style.

The ladies of the ICA attended courses in An Grianan, and organised fashion shows in the town. The tradition of holding public debates between the ladies of the ICA and the men of the Macra started a practice that still continues to provide great, often hilarious entertainment for one and all. In 1953, the Macra joined forces with the local ICA to give Abbeyleix its own annual Agricultural Show, and for the next thirty years the Show was to become one of the great events of the Midlands, drawing the best of show-jumpers and exhibitors from all over the country. While continuing to organise the Agricultural Show with members of Macra ne Feirme, many of the ICA ladies were involved in many other aspects of town life, the drama societies, the formation of bridge clubs, and in the development of the golf and tennis clubs.

There is no doubt that the ladies of the ICA along with their counterparts in Macra na Feirme have had a profound and innovative influence on the fabric of society in this town of ours. (*Images*: ICA members, 1984 (above); ICA members, 2000 (left).)

ABBEYLEIX TENNIS CLUB

ABBEYLEIX LAWN TENNIS CLUB, which recently celebrated its centenary in great style, has been one of the main centres of community activity, and a delightful focus for much of the social life in the town. From its foundation in 1909 in the town park, the tennis club has been blessed with generations of enthusiastic members ready and willing to become involved in the maintenance and development of the club. The site for the tennis club was a gift from Viscount de Vesci and the laying of the courts and building of the first clubhouse were carried out on a voluntary basis for the most part by the membership. In the early years, the surface of the courts consisted of sand compressed on to a gravel base. In the words of a reporter of the time, courts 'were of billiard-table level'. The marking of the court were of thin timber laths firmly pinioned to the ground. For the opening ceremony, over 100 guests arrived,

making it obvious from the start that this was an amenity that was going to be very popular. Throughout the 1920s and '30s, the tennis club developed steadily with an ever-increasing membership, putting pressure on facilities.

In 1935, with the permission and assistance of Viscount de Vesci, the club moved from its original site at the far corner of the town park to its present location, where a fine new clubhouse was erected and new courts were laid. When the new site was established, many matches were played over the years against the tennis clubs of surrounding towns with considerable success. Even more successful apparently were the after-match dances and social gatherings, a veritable ballroom of romance.

In modern times, Abbeyleix Lawn Tennis club is a shining example of success and achievement brought about by a vigorous community spirit and sense of belonging. A new clubhouse in 1989 and Edel Astroturf courts, laid in the early part of this century, complete with floodlighting, have made the club a leader among clubs, and one of which the whole town can be truly proud. A thriving juvenile and junior section suggests that the future of the club will be in good hands. Having celebrated the club's first 100 years in style in 2009, in the shade of the Centenary Gazebo, roll on the next 100 years. (*Images*: Abbeyleix Lawn Tennis Club. Opening Day, 1909 (below); Abbeyleix Lawn Tennis Club. Centenary Year, 2009 (left).)

ST LAZERIAN'S GAA CLUB

ON THE SPORTING front, the turn of the century
was a proud time for Abbeyleix. The Gaelic Athletic
Association had been founded in 1884, and such was
the interest and enthusiasm locally, that the first GAA
county convention was held in Abbeyleix in 1888. The
chairman was local man, John McMahon. The first
pitch used by St Lazerian's Hurling and Football Club,
as the Abbeyleix club was known, was at Coyle's field
in Ballymaddock, and the first recorded match was
a friendly against Durrow. The club was very strong
around the turn of the century, winning the County
Football Championship in 1889, and again in 1902,
1903, and 1904. It was in 1907 that the club was
affiliated as St Lazerian's Hurling and Football Club.
From about 1908 onwards, the hurling side of the club
was more prominent, and frequently provided many
players for the county team, including Ned McEvoy
who won his All-Ireland medal with Laois in 1915.

The hurling club was very successful for many years,

and won the senior County Hurling Championship six times during the 1930s and '40s.

These days, the club plays at senior level in hurling in the town park, their colours being saffron and blue. Many of the Abbeyleix players were part of the Ballyroan Gaels team, an amalgamation of the Abbeyleix and Ballyroan clubs. (*Images*: St Lazerian's Club, *c.* 1907 (above); St Lazerian's Club, 2007 (left).)

ABBEYLEIX ATHLETIC SOCCER CLUB

DURING WINTER MONTHS, from 1949 onwards, the members of the Old Estate Cricket Club started playing soccer which proved to be a more popular game and eventually took over completely from the cricket. Under the Management of Pat O'Brien, Abbeyleix Estate Soccer Club soon gained entry into the Kilkenny League and became one of the better teams, finishing near the top of the league more often than not. In those days, home matches were played on the gently

sloping pitch known as the Thatch Bog. The club jersey was blue and white, and a full set cost £10. As the years passed, the soccer club declined somewhat, until in 1967, it was revived at a public meeting in town and became Abbeyleix Athletic Soccer Club and played in the Carlow League with distinction for a number of years. Eventually the soccer club developed their pitch in the town park, and became a force to be reckoned with in Leinster League soccer.

Abbeyleix Athletic senior team has the longest history of continuous play of all teams currently playing in Laois. The club has three senior teams and 200 juvenile players. The senior teams play in the Combined Counties League while the juveniles play in the Midlands Schoolboys/girls League. The club has one full-sized pitch, an all-weather training pitch, and also uses the park's seven-a-side astroturf. The ambition of the club is to promote soccer in the area for all. The increasing numbers means that the club's priority is to acquire a second pitch to allow continuing development. (*Images: Abbeyleix Estate Soccer Club, 1950 (left); Abbeyleix Athletic Soccer Club, 2010 (above).*)

THE RAILWAY STATION

IN THE MID-1800S, two railway lines were developed very quickly: one connecting Waterford and Kilkenny was operational by 1845, and another linking Dublin with Cork was finished in 1849. In 1860, on the suggestion of Viscount de Vesci, a proposal to connect these two lines was accepted. Originally, the line was to come from Kilkenny to Attanagh, and through Abbeyleix to Mountrath. The first nineteen miles from Kilkenny to Abbeyleix was completed by 1865, but the scheme ran into difficulties, and it was a further two years before the work was completed, by which time it had been decided to take the line to Maryborough (now Portlaoise) rather than

Mountrath. The line was officially opened on 1 May 1867, complete with the elegant limestone station house.

The presence of the railway had an enormous influence on the life of the town and its hinterland, and was of great commercial and economic benefit to the area. The dark green engines with their light green trimmings, pouring out their mixture of steam and smoke to drift on the breeze, dramatically expanded the horizons of the ordinary people, as journeys, which by horse-drawn coach had taken days, could now be completed in hours. Quite suddenly, the big towns and cities, which for most people had been talked about but never seen, were within reach and could be visited within the length of one day.

In the 1920s, the station building was a victim of the Civil War in that it was burnt down. Fortunately, it was quickly rebuilt and returned to its former condition. In its own way the railway became the centre of great sadness as the tragedy of massive emigration began and continued throughout the second half of the century. So many heartbreaking farewells must have taken place on the limestone platforms of the station as many of our ancestors, left their kith and kin behind; many never to return.

Sadly, and despite much debate and negotiation, the railway line linking Portlaoise to Kilkenny through Abbeyleix was closed on 31 December 1962, amid much sadness and misgiving. The station goods yard became the home of a new industry, Stonearch Ltd. Inevitably too, Stonearch Ltd closed in recent years, leaving the station house as a private dwelling and the site of the rails as an expansive garden. (*Images*: Abbeyleix railway, *c*. 1960s (left); Abbeyleix Station House as it is today (above).)

ON THE ROADS

METHODS OF TRAVELLING around Abbeyleix changed dramatically as the years slipped by. Around 1944, life moved at a slower place and coming into town for the shopping depended generally on the donkey, commonly known as an ass, who pulled either a trap, which was a luxury item, or a basic cart.

Getting home during the age of the donkey was very easy, particularly in the late evening after a drink or two. Just untie the ass and sit in the cart or trap and the ass would find its own way home with very little input from the driver. Truly a breathalyzer free era.

In modern times, the motor car is king, considerably faster and more comfortable with shelter from the weather. It can be, however, much more stressful driving in traffic and getting in and out of a parking bay can be much more complicated. Such is progress. (*Images*: Coming into town, 1944 (left); Coming into town, 2011 (above).)

FOUNTAINS OF ABBEYLEIX

In all the town of Abbeyleix has five fountains, three of which are memorials and two were for practical use. In recent years all five have been restored and in their own quiet way add to the heritage character of the town.

The Northern Fountain
In the middle of the eighteenth-century the de Vesci family provided a piped water system for the town. The system was gravity fed and consequently was not available to the residents of the higher

reaches of Rathmoyle. This fountain was installed and connected to the main system to supply fresh water for these residents. After being removed when road improvements were being carried out during the 1980s, the fountain has since been restored to its former limestone glory in front of Heritage House.

The Market Square Fountain
This fountain is a memorial to the second Viscount de Vesci and was erected in appreciation of the assistance given by the de Vesci family to the local population during the Famine years when all rents were reduced and food distribution organised. It is in the shape of an obelisk on a rectangular plinth and was designed by J.S. Butler in 1860. Along with the town library it forms a focal point in the town centre.

The Southern Fountain

This fountain, which stands at the southern end of town, was commissioned by Lady Emma de Vesci in memory of her husband the third Viscount. It was designed in 1877 and was built by a Mr Sharpe of Dublin. The structure is Gothic in design built essentially of limestone and covered with some exquisite carvings, including one of the de Vesci Arms on the side facing the Durrow Road.

Ballacolla Road Fountain

This fountain known as the Wingfield Memorial fountain is situated on the Ballacolla Road near the entrance to the Church of Ireland Church. It commemorates Revd William Wingfield who served as vicar of Abbeyleix for forty-four years from 1836 to 1880. During his time in office he supervised the major reconstruction of the Church of Ireland church by the architect Sir Thomas Wyatt in the 1860s and witnessed many changes in his parish as the town grew and developed.

Balladine Fountain

This fountain appears to have been erected for the purpose of supplying fresh water to the residents of the townland of Balladine which straddles the Mountrath road out of town. It is a small limestone structure which for many years had been overgrown and forgotten. In recent years it has been restored and made operational. Originally the water depended on a gravity feed, but in modern times a pumping system is used and the whole structure is kept in pristine condition by local residents.

FESTIVALS OF ABBEYLEIX

Over the years many festivals of varying kinds have been held in the town for one reason or another. In some cases, they were part of national programs organised in times of economic hardship to give a source of encouragement to the population. Memories of three such festivals are summarised in this article.

An Tostal

This was a nationwide festival held during the mid-1950s. Each participating town received its An Tostal flag which was raised with great ceremony on a prominent flagpole in town and proudly flew for the fortnight of the program. The shops and premises were suitably decorated and the Abbeyleix St Brigid's Pipe Band paraded through the town for the opening and closing ceremonies and at various other functions. One of the many happy memories of An Tostal was the production of a souvenir booklet compiled by the secretary of the local An Tostal committee Mr. J. H. Harley. The booklet contained a series of historical narratives of the town and a selection of legendary stories of the area which provided great interest for all. Abbeyleix an Tostal was very successful and introduced the town as 'The Heart of the Irish in the Heart of Ireland' to local and visitor alike.

Abbeyleix Maytime Festival

In the 1980s, Abbeyleix Maytime Festival took over the town during the month of May and was a lavish affair. Under the guidance of James E. Cahill the festival committee organised and ran many events. A Festival Queen was chosen, a Festival Lord Mayor was elected by popular vote and both 'ruled' serenely for the duration of the program. An Open Week in the local Golf Club brought many visitors to the town for the festivities as did the Festival Song Contest, and the many marvellous concerts and dances held in the town. A major festival parade with colourful floats from businesses and organisations in the town filled the Main Street with excited and happy spectators. Abbeyleix was the place to be during the years of the Maytime Festival.

Abbeyfest

In recent years some enterprising and enthusiastic Abbeyleix folk have organised a new festival known as Abbeyfest. The program runs in June usually over the bank holiday weekend. The highlight of the festival is the Family Fun Day, usually on the Sunday, which presents some of the finest street entertainment in the country. Entertainment for children is very much at the heart of the Abbeyfest program. Presentations in Visual Arts and a series of shows on the Comedy Evening and many other functions ensure a weekend of first-class entertainment.

MYASTHENIA GRAVIS

The royalties from the sale of this book will be donated to the Myasthenia Gravis Association (MGA).

Myasthenia Gravis (MG) is an auto-immune disease in which the immune system attacks and damages the nerve signal reception areas. This causes a breakdown between nerves and muscles and results in loss of effectiveness in the muscles of the arms, legs and eyes. The name 'Myasthenia Gravis' comes from the Greek and Latin words for 'grave muscular weakness'.
MG occurs in all races, in both genders and at any age. It is not thought to be directly inherited, nor is it contagious. Occasionally, it occurs in more than one member of the same family. It most commonly affects young adult women (under forty) and older men (over sixty), but it can occur at any age. Research shows that 80 per cent of MG sufferers are over fifty-five; 13 per cent are between twenty-one and fifty-five and 7 per cent are under twenty-one.
   The MGA is the national charity for people with Myasthenia Gravis (or 'the Ragdoll Illness'), supporting and providing information to patients, raising awareness, and funding medical research. Our patron is Ronnie Whelan whose eldest daughter has the illness. Whether you are concerned about symptoms, have been newly diagnosed, know someone with the disease or are just curious, we are here to lend support directly and act as gateway.
   The MGA is a registered charity in both Ireland and the UK. The National Coordinator for Ireland is Karen Clancy, based in Co. Clare.

Myasthenia Gravis Association (Ireland)
Lavalla
Ballynacally
Ennis
Co. Clare

karen.clancy@mga-charity.ie
www.mga-charity.ie
tel: 065-6838270 / 087-4160385

If you enjoyed this book, you may also be interested in ...

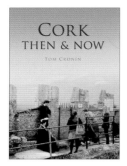

Cork Then & Now
TOM CRONIN

The popular tourist city of Cork has a rich heritage, which is uniquely reflected in this fascinating new compilation. Contrasting a selection of forty-five archive images alongside full-colour modern photographs, this book delves into the changing faces and buildings of this historic county. Comparing the workers of yesteryear with today's modern men and women, along with some famous landmarks and little-known street scenes, this is a wide-ranging look at the city's colourful history.

978 1 84588 725 4

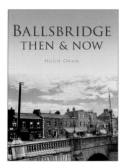

Ballsbridge Then & Now
HUGH ORAM

Ballsbridge, the 'embassy belt' at the leafy heart of South Dublin, is home to the Royal Dublin Society (RDS), the British and American embassies, the Aviva Stadium, and an array of the great houses of Ireland. Aside from the area's conspicuous grandeur, it is also steeped in history. Herbert Park was the site of the visit of King George V and throughout its wide streets are statues and mementos of the great moments of the Irish state. This book captures the changing face of one of the most striking parts of all Ireland.

978 1 84588 726 1

Haunted Kilkenny
CORMAC STRAIN

Modern tales of poltergeists in housing estates, phantom voices, ghostly nannies, white ladies and banshees - this isn't the stuff of oft-repeated folklore; these are freshly discovered ghostly tales from the people of Kilkenny. Ideal for the paranormal enthusiast, the local historian, the Kilkenny diaspora abroad and anyone who enjoys a good, scary story, *Haunted Kilkenny* is a book for everyone.

978 1 84588 748 3

Athlone Miscellany
GEAROID O'BRIEN

This a collection of the historical articles published by Gearoid O'Brien, author, historian and broadcaster have always had a wide readership, and are known for capturing a sense of the town and the community, in an informative and engaging way. Originally appearing in the *Westmeath Independent*, this is the first time these articles have been published together, and represent a valuable history of the changing face of Athlone

978 1 84588 709 4

Visit our website and discover thousands of other History Press books.

www.thehistorypress.ie